THE
RUDIMENTS OF
GENTEEL BEHAVIOR

Francis Nivelon

Paul Holberton publishing

php

Facsimile edition of François Nivelon,
The Rudiments of Genteel Behavior, London 1737,
by Paul Holberton publishing 2003

Foreword by Paul Holberton
© Paul Holberton 2003
Afterword by Hugh Belsey
© Hugh Belsey 2003
Photograph p. 69
Photographic Survey, Courtauld Institute of Art

ISBN 1 903470 1 0 2

British Library Cataloguing in Publication Data
A catalogue record for this book is available from the British Library

Produced by
Paul Holberton publishing, 37 Snowsfields, London SE1 3SU
www.paul-holberton.net

Designed by Roger Davies
daviesdesign@onetel.net.uk

Printed in Italy

Distributed in UK, Europe and the rest of the world by Greenhill Books
Distributed in USA and Canada by University of Washington Press
Internet sales at www.paul-holberton.net

THE
RUDIMENTS
OF
GENTEEL BEHAVIOR
BY
F. Nivelon.
1737.

L.P.Boitard Fecit.

FOREWORD

H E Rudiments of Genteel Behavior is difficult to classify. You could be forgiven for consigning it to the vast and dated category of literature known as 'courtesy books', which from the Middle Ages to the twentieth century prescribed or advised the budding monarch, the courtier, or the would-be man or woman of society how to behave – guides to good conduct, in which, in the past at least, there was invariably a weighty moral component. But such a component is entirely and unusually absent here. On the other hand courtesy literature certainly recognizes the importance of 'genteel behaviour', the kind of 'deportment' so precisely described in *The Rudiments*: courtiers and gentlemen were always to be good at riding and dancing and showing a leg as well as learning and fighting. Although *The Rudiments* is exclusively concerned with appearance and movement – how to stand, how to curtsey, how to doff your hat – it emphasizes that crucial to the successful enactment of these basics is a quality very like 'dispreciation' or *sprezzatura*, that great art of making whatever you do look easy and natural, which is exemplified by the model of all early modern courtesy books, Castiglione's sixteenth-century *Courtier*. The fourth Lord Chesterfield, whose earliest letters of admonition and example to his son and godson are exactly contemporary with *The Rudiments*, not only urged, besides physical and intellectual exercise, the arts of dancing and fencing, but repeated: "Remember there is another great object that must keep pace with, and accompany, knowledge; I mean Manners, Politeness, and the Graces ... I repeat, and shall never cease repeating to you, *the Graces, the Graces*".

These 'graces', and the 'airs' that accompany them, have of course fallen out of the fashion they once epitomized, and into the purgatory of affectation, of show and sham and of being what one isn't. That can only be the result, not simply of changing notions of what is natural, but of far too many people trying to attain "a graceful attitude, and agreeable motion, and easy air and a genteel behaviour" – as the subtitle of Nivelon's book claims to teach (and which was taken as the title of a plagiarized new edition, with rather poorer engravings, that appeared not many years afterwards). Despite the evident need in 1737, at the height of the Rococo period, for instruction in an "easy disposition", such as Nivelon urges his "willing Learner" to "observe well" in the figure of his second plate, copies of *The Rudiments of Genteel Behaviour* are now extremely rare (its plagiarized version seems to be even rarer); the example reproduced here, bought in 2002 from the London antiquarian book dealer Simon Finch for Gainsborough's House in Sudbury (Suffolk, England), is claimed to be only the eighth known in the world.

Was *The Rudiments* a failure? Was its marketing compromised by the death of Nivelon's brother in a duel in Paris in 1738, which perhaps required him to return to France? Or was its purpose to be no more than a 'calling card' that would help establish the dancing school that Francis, his distinguished career on the London stage now over, set up in Stamford in Lincolnshire in 1739? It seems, perhaps, too lavish a production for such a purpose – it was surely a labour of love, as Hugh Belsey suggests in his Afterword – too ample and grand in text and illustration to be a mere manual, and perhaps not actually very useful for a débutante or younger son about to enter the marriage market. Its amplitude and grandeur were clearly intended to reflect the gentility and grace with which the author is minutely concerned. Such exactitude cannot be found in any other historical source: no other source will tell you so particularly, for example, how to hold, raise and lower your hat as Nivelon does in his second plate for the male figure, 'WALKING and SALUTING passing by'. Such is the precision of the text and of its relation to the image that Nivelon must have commissioned the paintings by Bartholomew Dandridge on which the engravings are based (for which perhaps he originally found use in the premises of his dancing school). Although by 1737 Hogarth was already active, and had recently founded his St Martin's Lane academy, Dandridge was a leading painter, with an aristocratic clientèle, and it seems from the survival of two loose engravings (see Afterword) that for the reproduction of his work Nivelon intended to employ Hubert François Gravelot, certainly the finest printmaker of his day, though his compatriot Louis Philippe Boitard, whom he eventually used, also did a good job.

The quality of the engravings, together with the unusual precision both of the images and of the text, make the book remarkable – and again in this respect quite unlike the ordinary run of courtesy book, which, when illustrated, is illustrated rather poorly. Not only its charm but the ambition of the book is striking: Nivelon, after a career of twenty years' acclaim on the London stage, clearly believed, perhaps with justified Gallic confidence, since the prestige of French art – and dancing – was at its height at this moment, that he had particular knowledge of what gentility really was. He recognized at any rate – a sign of his times – that it could become a commodity.

Paul Holberton

REFERENCES

For courtesy books in general, see J.E. Mason, *Gentlefolk in the Making: Studies in the History of English Courtesy Literature and related topics 1531 to 1774*, Philadelphia 1935.
The quotation from Lord Chesterfield is from letter 106 to his son, cited after Georges Lemoine, 'Lord Chesterfield's *Letters* as Conduct-Books', in *The Crisis of Courtesy: Studies in the Conduct-Book in Britain, 1600–1900*, ed. Jacques Carré, Leyden 1994, pp. 105–17, at p. 112.
For the rarity of Nivelon's work see Simon Finch Rare Books, London, Catalogue 50, p. 94, no. 142. However, one more copy is in the National Art Library in the Victoria and Albert Museum, and features in facsimile in the recently installed British Galleries there.

THE

RUDIMENTS

OF

GENTEEL BEHAVIOR

BY

F. Nivelon.

L.P.Boitard Fecit.

INTRODUCTION

TO THE

Method of attaining a graceful Attitude, an agreeable Motion, an eafy Air, and a genteel Behaviour

HE Head. being the principal Part of the human Figure, muft be firft confider'd, becaufe it entirely governs all the Reft, and when properly fituated, erect and free, the Neck will appear in its true Proportion, the Shoulders will retain their proper Places, the Cheft will grow broad and full, and the Breaft round, the Back will be ftraight and light, and affiftant to the Motion of the Hipps, they to the Motion of the Knees, and the Knees, in like Manner, to the Feet.

INTRODUCTION.

But if the Head be improperly fituated, by projecting forward, it fpoils the true Proportion of the Neck, which can never be remedied by faftning Collars or Bandages to draw it back (a Cuftom too prevalent in the Infancy of the Female Sex) but on the contrary, by confining the Neck in fuch a Manner, it is not only painful to it, but of bad Confequence, for it is thereby deprived of due Nourifhment, and the free Communication between the Head and Body is greatly obftructed; the Shoulders too, by a Head fo placed, are drawn out of their proper Places, which certainly renders the Cheft narrow, and the Breaft, becoming hollow, reftrains the Freedom of Breathing, the Back grows heavy and burthenfome to the Hipps, they to the Knees, and the Knees to the Feet.

And as a Perfon, whofe Head is rightly placed, is capable of Standing, Walking, Dancing, or performing any genteel Exercife in a graceful, eafy and becoming Manner; the Perfon, whofe Head is wrong placed, is wholly incapable of Standing, Walking, Dancing, or performing any Exercife but with Difficulty, and in a Manner very aukward and unbecoming.

I fhall next confider the Feet as of great Importance to the Air, Grace and Motion of the human Figure; if they are turn'd inwards, the Hipps will feem heavy and mifplaced, but if turn'd outwards will appear firm, yet light and eafy. The Heels fhould be rather low than high, for if low, the Eafe, Strength and true Proportion of the Perfon is preferved; if high they cannot be eafy or fafe, but on the contrary will deftroy the Strength and true Proportion of the Limbs, by ftraining the Infteps and Ancles, and forcing the Knees forward in fuch a Manner as will prevent ftanding or moving upright, but in pain and fear of falling at every Step, as is too obvious in many of the Fair Sex, to whom, in compliance with the

cuftomary

INTRODUCTION.

cuſtomary Complaiſance uſed by Perſons of Politeneſs, the Preference in the following Deſcriptions muſt be given.

For a further and better Explanation, Recourſe muſt be had to the following Figures, which, with their Deſcriptions, will fully inſtruct the willing Learner in the RUDIMENTS of GENTEEL BEHAVIOUR.

And firſt to deſcribe the true Way to make the COURTSIE.

The COURTSIE.

T H E Head muſt be erect, the Shoulders drawn back, the Arms ſideways, neither forwards nor backwards but eaſy, as in this Figure, not too cloſe to the Body, for if ſo they would hide the Shape and appear aukward. The Hands placed a-croſs not high or low, but to the Point of the Shape, the Inſide of the Hands ſhould be oppoſed to the Breaſt, the Fingers being eaſy and a little ſeparated, the Wriſts muſt bend inwards, but not ſo much as to make the Arms appear Lame, and conſequently diſagreeable; keep firm upon the Limbs from the Hipps downwards, then turn with eaſe, and looking at the Perſon or Perſons to whom the Complement is intended, take a Step ſideways with either Foot and join the other to it; let the Eyes (being downcaſt, as this Figure deſcribes) diſcover Humility and Reſpect, whilſt bending not too much, but moderately, you make the COURTSIE properly; then riſing from it gradually raiſe the Eyes ſo too, and look with becoming Modeſty.

B. Dandridge Pinx.   L. P. Boitard Sculp.

According to Act of Parliament.

THE

SECOND FIGURE

Defcribes the moft genteel Manner of

Giving or Receiving any Thing.

To GIVE or RECEIVE.

 BSERVE well the eafy Difpofition of this Figure, and in that Manner approach with becoming Modefty and gentle Motion, not too near, nor Stop at too great Diftance, for the one will oblige the Perfon you addrefs, to retire, the other to advance, both which will be wrong, and therefore muft be avoided, and the proper Diftance kept, then make the COURTSIE in Manner as defcribed in the firft Figure, and, as about to Deliver or Receive, prefent the Right Hand, and withdraw it a little, then prefenting it again, GIVE or RECEIVE the Thing intended, and eafily withdrawing the Hand, till it comes to a circular Action, place it on the other, as defcribed in the preceding Figure, and COURTSIE as before; and if you quit the Place walk gently, and again COURTSIE at the Door, or fome little Diftance from the Perfon GIVING or RECEIVING.

Plate 2.

B. Dandridge Pinx.   L. P. Boitard Sculp.

According to Act of Parliament.

THE

THIRD FIGURE

Defcribes the proper Manner of

WALKING.

WALKING.

THE Head muſt be erect and free to move, the Body alſo upright, diſengag'd and eaſy, the Arms to the Point of the Elbow likewiſe falling gracefully, and the Hands a-croſs, as deſcribed in this Figure; the Step muſt be in Proportion to the Height, the Leg that moves foremoſt muſt come to the Ground with a ſtrait Knee, and the Body will infenſibly move to that and leave the other Leg light and free to paſs forward in like Manner, at which Time, looking with decent Humility, and a ſubmiſſive Air, the Courtsie in paſſing by may be properly made by joining the backward Foot to that which is foremoſt, and ſinking and riſing gradually, then Walk as before. It is neceſſary to obſerve that it will be impracticable to Dance, or perform any genteel Action or Exerciſe, without attaining this Method of Walking, which this Figure proves to be right; for though from the Waiſt to the Feet the Limbs are not diſcover'd, yet the Foot advanc'd ſtanding firm and turn'd outwards, proves that Knee to be ſtrait, whereas if the Foot was otherwiſe, the Knee would be ſo too, and it is impoſſible without being ſtrait on the advanc'd Knee, to Walk well, eaſy, or graceful.

Plate 3.

B. Dandridge Pinx.

L. P. Boitard Sculp.

According to Act of Parliament

T H E different Attitudes of the three Figures before mention'd, being duly drawn from the Life, and the juſt Proportions ſtrictly obſerved, are therefore worthy Notice and Imitation, which by a little Practice (without other Aſſiſtance) may fully Inſtruct in the Manner of genteel Motion and Behaviour; and having attained that Foundation, a Perſon may learn to Dance, and improve therein, in a ſhort Time, and without Difficulty; for when the graceful Attitude and eaſy Motion of Body and Limbs are known and perform'd, Dancing may be learn'd with more than ten times the Eaſe to both Maſter and Scholar, and in leſs than a tenth Part of the Time that it will require without ſuch a proper Introduction.

The Fourth Figure, with ſome Explanation, will deſcribe the proper Behaviour in Dancing.

DANCING.

EEP the Head not quite upright, but incline it a little with graceful Motion and all imaginable Eafe; let the Eyes appear lively and modeft, and the Face exprefs neither Mirth nor Gravity, but the Medium, which will form an amiable Mein and always be agreeable; the Neck to the Shoulders, and from them to the Elbows and Wrifts are truly proportion'd, and a genteel Attitude plainly fhewn in this Figure; each Forefinger and Thumb muft hold the Petticoat, and the other Fingers be a little feparated; the Body fhould have a little Swing in its Motion, juft to avoid the Appearance of Stiffnefs, and let the Feet appear well turn'd and without any Affectation, as in this Figure, which fhews certainly the proper Behaviour in DANCING, it appearing from Head to Foot modeft, light and eafy.

Plate 4.

R. Dandridge Pinx.

L.P. Boitard Sculp.

According to Act of Parliament.

T H E

FIFTH FIGURE

Will be affifting to the Defcription of

Giving a HAND in a MINUET.

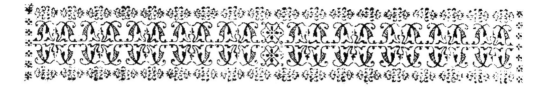

Giving a HAND in a MINUET.

THE Body muft reft on the left Foot light and graceful, the Head muft be turn'd free, and the Eyes look over the right Wrift at the Partner, the Shoulders remaining eafy, the Arm bending a little Circular and at the fame Diftance from the Body, as by this Figure, in Proportion, is exprefs'd; for if the Hand be near the Body, the Elbow will project out fharp and the Wrift appear lame; the Fingers muft not be clofed nor too far feparated, the Forefinger and Thumb (tho' near each other) muft not join, nor the little Finger point out as if it had no Joints; the Arm muft not fwing, nor the Wrift have a twifting Motion, but the Hand rifing from the Petticoat, with graceful Eafe, muft appear as you obferve in this Figure, then give the Hand, and on withdrawing it bend the Arm as before and let it fall eafy as it was rais'd, and in the Time that falls raife the other in like Manner.

This Figure alfo fhews the right Foot properly turn'd outwards in the Action of taking a *Contre Temps*, which is bending, rifing, and fliding.

Plate 5.

B. Dandridge Pinx.   L.P. Boitard Sculp.

According to Act of Parliament.

THE

SIXTH FIGURE

Defcribes the Manner of

Giving both HANDS in a MINUET.

Giving both HANDS in a MINUET.

I N the preceding Figure, one Hand is offer'd, in this both ; the Arms muſt not come ſuddenly to that Attitude, but with eaſy, graceful Motion without ſtopping ; this Figure ſhews how high the Arms muſt riſe before the Hands turn to the Hands of the Partner ; the circular Action of both Arms is an Expreſſion of Civility till the Hands are turn'd into thoſe of the Partner ; let the Looks and Actions, during the Dance, be wholly addreſs'd to the Partner ; keep Time in an eaſy Motion ; avoid being too near the Partner in the Dance, but finiſh it without hurry ; paying the uſual Reſpects to the Company and the Partner, and parting in an eaſy, obliging Manner, which will pleaſe more than the Dance itſelf ; on the contrary, if the Dance be finiſh'd, and the Parting made in a haſty, careleſs Manner, it will Merit Cenſure, rather than Applauſe.

Plate 6.

THESE Defcriptions of what is proper to be imitated and practifed before, and in, and at the finifhing the Dance, and the Cautions to avoid what is unbecoming and improper, has been carefully ftudied, and is hereby recommended to the ftrict Obfervance of thofe among the Fair Sex, who had rather be, and appear, eafy, amiable, genteel and free in their Perfon, Mein, Air and Motions, than ftiff, aukward, deform'd and, confequently, difagreeable.

A S the Exteriour Part of the human Figure gives the firſt Impreſſion, it will be no unpleaſing Task to adorn that with the amiable Qualities of Decency and genteel Behaviour, which to accompliſh, it will be abſolutely neceſſary to aſſiſt the Body and Limbs with Attitudes and Motions eaſy, free and graceful, and thereby diſtinguiſh the polite Gentleman from the rude Ruſtick. The following Figures, in which are deſcribed and delineated various Actions of the Gentleman in genteel Behaviour, being taken from the Life, and the true Proportions ſtrictly preſerv'd, will, with the Aſſiſtance of a little Deſcription, ſufficiently demonſtrate that thoſe agreeable Faculties may, by a curious Obſervance and pleaſing Study of them, be ſpeedily attained and practiſed without the tedious Introduction too common in learning the Art of Dancing.

Without further Prelude I ſhall proceed, as in the former Part of the Book to examine and deſcribe the Gentleman in the following Figures.

The firſt of which may be properly called the Foundation of all Exerciſe, that is to STAND firm, yet eaſy and without Affectation.

STANDING.

THE Head erect and turnd, as in this Figure, will be right, as will the manly Boldnefs in the Face, temper'd with becoming Modefty; the Lips muft be juft join'd to keep the Features regular; the Shoulders muft fall eafy, and be no farther drawn back than to form the Cheft full and round, which will preferve the true Proportion of the Body, but if they are too far drawn back, the Cheft will appear to prominent, the Arms ftiff and lame, and the Back hollow, which will intirely fpoil the true Proportion, and therefore muft be carefully avoided ; the Arms muft fall eafy, not clofe to the Sides, and the Bend of the Elbow, at its due Diftance, will permit the right Hand to place itfelf in the Waiftcoat eafy and genteel, as in this Figure is reprefented ; but any rifing or falling the Hand from that Place, will make it appear lame, and confequently difagrecable; the Hat fhou'd be plac'd eafy under the left Arm, and that Wrift muft be free and ftrait, and the Hand fupport itfelf above the Sword-hilt; the Sword exactly plac'd as fhewn in this Figure, is the only proper and genteel Situation for it; the whole Body muft reft on the right Foot, and the right Knee, as alfo the Back be kept ftraight; the left Leg muft be foremoft, and only bear its own weight, and both Feet muft be turn'd outwards, as fhewn by this Figure, neither more or lefs, but exactly.

Plate 2.

According to Act of Parliament

THE SECOND FIGURE is intended to ſhew the proper Manner of Walking, and paying the Complement of taking off the Hat paſſing by; and as many of the Gentlemen of dignified Stations in the Army do retain the moſt manly, yet eaſy and genteel Attitudes and Motions, the following Figure is deſigned to repreſent in one of their Officers, the Gentleman Walking and paying the Complement abovemention'd.

WALKING and SALUTING paffing by.

IN Walking, the Perfon muſt be erect, not inclining backwards, the advanc'd Knee muſt be ſtrait, the Step moderate, and the whole Body and Limbs diſengag'd, and free to move gracefully; the right Arm muſt riſe to the Hat with moderate Motion ſideways, the Wriſt muſt be ſtrait, the Hand turn'd and its Palm ſhewn, the Fingers muſt be on the Brim, and the Forefinger extended on the Crown of the Hat, and the Thumb under the Brim (near the Forehead) which preſerves the Shape and Faſhion; and whilſt taking it off, let the Look and Action be complaiſantly addreſs'd to the Perfon to whom the Complement is intended; the left Arm ſhould fall neither backward nor forward (both which wou'd look diſagreeable) but gently by the Side, diſcovering the Inſide, and holding the Glove in an eaſy, careleſs Manner; then being firm on the left Leg, the right will be at liberty to advance and make the Bow on the right Side; but if the Perfon to be addreſs'd be on the left Side, the right Leg muſt be firm and the left advance to perform the Complement.

Plate 2.

B.Dandridge Pinx.   L.P.Boitard Sculp.

According to Act of Parliament.

THE

THIRD FIGURE

Reprefents the genteel Manner of

Making the B O W with the Hat off.

The B O W

T H É preceding Figure reprefented the right Hand ready to take off the Hat, and this Figure fhews it taken off. The Hand appears to hold the Hat as in the preceding Defcription, the infide of the Hat muft be difcovered, for if the outfide, was fhewn the Arm wou'd feem lame ; both Arms muft advance with freedom, the Head a little inclining forwards to the Object of Addrefs? the Eyes a little downcaft at the Time of the Complement, will fhew Refpect, which cannot be fhewn looking at the Perfon ; the left Leg (which in the laft Figure appears firm, and fupports the whole Body) bends in this Figure, which affifts the right Leg to advance freely and make the Bow ; but if the Perfon addrefs d be on the left Side, the right Leg muft bend, and the left advance to perform the Complement ; then in recovering the Bow the Body muft rife on the advanc'd Leg, which will leave the other free to pafs, and properly replacing the Hat, Walk as before in an eafy, graceful Manner.

Plate 3.

B.Dandridge Pinx.   L.P. Boitard Sculp.

According to Act of Parliament.

IT is an Obfervation (which cannot efcape Notice) that many Perfons retiring, or taking leave of any Perfon or Company, either thro' want of Knowledge or Neglect in difcovering a decent Carriage at their Departure, have appear'd very aukward Figures to Perfons of polite Behaviour; therefore this FOURTH FIGURE is defign'd to reprefent the Complement in RETIRING, and the proper Defcription of it may inform fuch carelefs Perfons how to demean themfelves for the future in this particular.

The Complement RETIRING.

BE firm on the right Foot with a ſtrait Knee to ſhew the Shape of the Leg in the beſt Manner, the left Leg turn'd, as in this Figure, with the Knee ſtrait and the Foot reſting lightly on it's Ball, the Heel not touching the Ground; then by Degrees and equal Motion the Knee muſt bend, and the left Leg be eaſily drawn back, and the Heel coming to the Ground the Body muſt recover on that Leg, and give the right Leg liberty to move; the Body muſt be quite eaſy, the Head inclining forwards, the Eyes downcaſt at the Time of Bowing, and raiſed as the Head riſes, then look with becoming Modeſty at the Perſon or Company and retire, inclining the Body the Way you go, for if otherwiſe it will confuſe and ſpoil the intended Complement; one Bow is enough in RETIRING, and many are rather troubleſome than obliging, by compelling a Return of ſuperfluous Complements.

Plate 4.

B. Dandrige Pinx: L. P. Boitard Sculp.

According to Act of Parliament.

T is a neceſſary Accompliſhment in a young Gentleman to attain (with an agreeable Diſpoſition of Body and Limbs) the proper Manner of OFFERING or RECEIVING. This FIFTH FIGURE, with its Deſcription, is therefore intended to ſhew the true and eaſy Manner of performing this Complement.

To Offfr or Receive.

THE Head, and the Body to the Waiſt, muſt incline forwards in a circular, eaſy Motion, and the Body muſt reſt on the left Leg, that Knee bending, the right Knee ſtrait, and the Ball of that Foot lightly touching the Ground; the right Arm muſt bend at the Wriſt and Elbow to appear a little Circular, as this Figure expreſſes, but at the Time of Offering or Receiving, the Arm muſt be extended, and the Look directed to the Hand offer'd to, or receiving from, then draw the Hand back, and a little Circular, as above deſcribed, and from that Attitude let it fall gently into its proper Place; the left Arm ſhould fall gently by the Side, holding the Hat in a careleſs, light, and eaſy Manner. If you ſtay, draw the right Leg ſideways, riſe upon the left Foot and ſtand firm; if you retire, raiſe the Body and draw the right Foot behind the left, which will finiſh the Bow properly for retreating with becoming Decency; it is alſo proper to uſe the left Leg in the ſame Manner as the right in advancing or retiring, the right, at the ſame Time, performing the Actions of the left, as abovemention d.

Plate 5.

B. Dandridge Pinx.

G.P. Boitard Sculp.

According to Act of Parliament.

THE Sixth and Last Figure is defign'd to fhew the proper Habit, Attitudes and agreeable Movements ufed in Dancing the Minuet, and fo to conclude this T R E A T I S E with that Defcription.

Dancing the Minuet.

TH E Hat (of a proper Size and Fashion) shou'd be plac'd firm, yet eafy on the Head, fo as to cover the Eyebrows, and the Point turning, fo as to be directly above the left Eye. In performing the Minuet, the Look, with becoming Modefty, muft be directed to the Partner; the right Arm muft rife with a fmooth, eafy Motion, the left Arm rife in the fame Time fideways at the Diftance, as (in Proportion) is fhewn by this Figure, the right Arm muft bend at the Elbow and Wrift, with the Fingers a little feparated, and the Palms of both Hands fhewn (as in this Figure) and it is to be obferved, that by raifing the left Arm in Manner as the right is above defcribed, the proper Action of giving both Hands in a Minuet is to be perform'd, and not otherwife ; and the Body being erect and refting on the left Foot. gives the right Foot (which lightly refts on its Ball) the eafy and genteel Movement in Dancing.

Plate 6.

B. Dandridge Pinx.   L. P. Boitard Sculp.

According to Act of Parliament.

AFTERWORD

N THE preface to his English translation of Pierre Rameau's 1725 *Maître à Danser*, published in 1728, John Essex tells us that dancing was "the peculiar Genius of the French Nation".[1] Despite its apparently different slant, this little 1737 *opus* of the French dancer François Nivelon, which he published after a highly successful career on the London stage, in many ways recalls such treatises, which had first appeared at the beginning of the century: Essex acknowledges the work of John Weaver, "the first that translated Monsieur Feuillet, concerning the Writing down of Dances in character, into the English language", in 1706.[2] With tools such as these becoming available and with the popularity of dance on stage increasing, by the middle of the century professional dancing masters were established in towns throughout England.[3] Corresponding to the claim of Nivelon's book to teach "genteel behaviour", their task was not merely to inculcate the steps of the minuet, it was also to provide instruction in deportment and conduct, or, as John Essex put it, to "qualify Persons, of what Condition soever," both to dance and to attain "a good Carriage and genteel Behaviour in Con versation" ('conversation' including not merely talk but mixing generally in society).[4]

Even those of the highest condition needed instruction. Philip, 4th Earl of Chesterfield, wrote to his son in 1748: "Dear Boy … I would have you dance [a minuet] very well. Remember, that the graceful motion of the arms, the giving your hand, and the putting-on and pulling-off your hat genteelly, are the material parts of a gentleman's dancing. But the greatest advantage of dancing well is, that it necessarily teaches you to present yourself, to sit, stand, and walk genteely, all which are of real importance to a man of fashion."[5] William Hogarth, too, in his 1753 *Analysis of Beauty*, bracketted deportment and dancing in his discussion of beauty "in action". Clearly, he says, "There is no one but would wish to have it in his power to be genteel and graceful in the carriage of his person, could it be attained with little trouble and expence of time. The usual methods relied on for this purpose among well-bred people, takes up a considerable part of their time: nay even those of the first rank have no other recourse in these matters, than to dancing-masters, and fencing-masters: dancing and fencing are undoubtedly proper, and very necessary accomplishments; yet are they frequently very imperfect in bringing about the business of graceful deportment. For altho' the muscles of the body may attain a pliancy by these exercises, and the limbs, by the elegant movement in dancing, acquire a facility in moving gracefully, yet for want of knowing the meaning of every grace, and whereon it depends, affectations and misapplications often follow." He had already indicated the likelihood of affectation in depicting the dancing-master in *The Rake's Progress* (fig. 1). As he sagely continues in *The Analysis of Beauty*, "Action is a sort of language which perhaps one time or other, may come to be taught by a kind of grammar-rules; but, at present, is only got by rote and imitation: and contrary to most other copyings and imitations, people of rank and fortune generally excel their originals, the dancing-masters, in easy behaviour and unaffected grace; as a sense of superiority makes them act without constraint; especially when their persons are well turn'd." Implicitly perhaps Hogarth condemns Francis Nivelon's book, *The Rudiments of Genteel Behavior*, as a failure, even though it is concerned not only with "rote and imitation"

1. William Hogarth (1697–1764)
A Rake's Progress II: Surrounded by Artists and Professionals, ca. 1733
Oil on canvas, 62.2 × 74.9 cm (24 1/2 × 29 1/2 in.)
Sir John Soane's Museum, London

Hogarth shows his famous wastrel, the young John Rakewell, in the company of a musician –
who resembles Handel – a jockey, a fencing master, a poet, a milliner, a tailor and, in the centre, a
dancing master, shown in profile to accentuate his strutting gait. There is a tradition that the figure
is a portrait of the most famous of contemporary dancing masters, John Essex (see text). Essex
reputedly also appears in one of the illustrations to Hogarth's *Analysis of Beauty*, published twenty
years later.

– in the precise detail which he provides about each posture – but also with "a kind of grammar-rules", or the principles behind deportment.

Francis (or François) was the younger and more talented son of Louis Nivelon, who had performed as a dancer in London around 1700. His sons, Louis and Francis, danced at the Paris Opéra before moving to London in October 1723, when they performed together at the theatre in Lincoln's Inn Fields. Francis continued to appear in pantomime in John Rich's company until 1728, when he returned to France. A contemporary commentator described his performance in *Achmet and Almanzine* as "admirable adroitness, all lightness and elegance, even in the most burlesque and contorted attitudes. Far from showing the slightest effort he seems to have endowed all his motions with grace."[7] In 1729 he returned to Lincoln's Inn Fields, where, amongst many other engagements, he danced *Harlequin Horace*, a satire on John Rich, partnered by Mrs John Laguerre: the poorly drawn frontispiece to the published text shows them performing arm in arm.[8] He was successful financially, earning as much as £5 a week, for the time a good income, which he was able to supplement with receipts from annual benefit appearances. In October 1733 he joined Theophilus Cibber's company at the Haymarket Theatre and occasionally appeared at the theatres at Richmond and Goodman's Fields before moving with Cibber to Drury Lane. In 1734/35 he joined John Rich's Covent Garden Theatre and gave interlude dances between the acts of plays performed there. In these he was often accompanied by pupils, so *The Rudiments of Genteel Behavior* was based on teaching experience. Soon after its publication in 1737 he learnt of the death of his second brother in a duel and he appears to have returned to Paris to sort out his family affairs. On his return in 1739 he is recorded in Stamford, Lincolnshire, where he set up a dancing school. The date of his death is not known.

Nivelon begins the book by stating his intention. He wants his readers to attain "a graceful Attitude, an agreeable Motion, an easy Air, and a genteel

66

2. Hubert François Gravelot (1699–1773)
Woman walking, ca. 1736
Engraving
Bibliothèque Nationale, Paris

3. Hubert François Gravelot
Man retiring, ca. 1736
Engraving
Bibliothèque Nationale, Paris

Hubert François Gravelot, having trained with François Boucher, settled in London in 1732, and taught at Hogarth's St Martin's Lane Academy from 1734. He was the finest draughtsman and engraver of his age, his work being appreciated both by several London publishers and by the younger generation of artists who learned from him, notable among them Thomas Gainsborough. These isolated engravings, evidently related to Francis Nivelon's project, anticipate a number of superb costume studies that were engraved by others after his designs in 1744 and 1745.

Behaviour", paying special attention to "the Head … the principal Part of the human Figure [which] governs all the Rest" of the body. The reader is told that if the head is wrongly placed, "the Person … is wholly incapable of Standing, Walking, Dancing, or performing any Exercise but with Difficulty, and in a Manner very aukward and unbecoming". He next considers the feet, which are "of great Importance to the Air, Grace and Motion of the human Figure; if they are turn'd inwards, the Hipps will seem heavy and misplaced, but if turn'd outward will appear firm, yet light and easy". He then cites twelve examples which demonstrate the route towards genteel behaviour. Each of the twelve positions, six each for a man and a woman, are illustrated with engravings by Louis Philippe Boitard, who based his design on paintings by Bartholomew Dandridge.

The book is written with precision and shows a command of language that has led other commentators to suggest that Nivelon may have been assisted by a native English speaker.[9] His concern in using precise language is reflected in his desire to use effective illustrations. Hubert François Gravelot, a fellow Frenchman and one of the foremost engravers in London, produced two prints for the book using Dandridge's paintings as models (figs. 2 and 3). They resemble Boitard's illustrations of a woman 'Walking' and a man giving 'The Compliment Retiring'.[10] Both figures stand on a terrace with elaborate garden backgrounds beyond – which Nivelon may have felt were a distraction from the purpose of the book. A portraitist who painted both full-scale figures and conversation pieces on a scale larger than usual, Dandridge no doubt painted the twelve canvases, like many of his other works, with landscape backgrounds, and Nivelon may have felt that they needed some adaptation before being used as illustrations for his book. The most likely hypothesis is that Dandridge's paintings were a separate commission, perhaps for Nivelon's dancing rooms in London and Stamford, and that the designs were used only as a basis for the book. Perhaps Gravelot was given an insufficient

4. Arthur Devis (1712–1787)
Lady and Gentleman in a Landscape, later 1740s
Oil on canvas, 71.1 × 91.4 cm (28 × 36 in.)
Wimpole Hall, The Bambridge Collection (The National Trust)

The pinched figures of Arthur Devis's conversation pieces are often cast in poses Nivelon chose to illustrate. Devis frequently painted aspiring gentry (unfortunately the identity of this particular couple is lost), of the kind that Nivelon presumably aimed to inform. In this portrait the gentleman, his attention momentarily caught by the viewer, receives a gift of symbolic honeysuckle that his new wife proffers, both in poses like those proscribed by Nivelon, 'To Give or Receive' and 'To Offer or Receive', female and male. Honeysuckle, a sweet-smelling climber dependant on its support, was frequently used as a symbol of marriage in paintings during the eighteenth century.

brief and after his disappointment the restless Nivelon turned to Boitard to carry out the commission. Unfortunately, none of Dandridge's paintings has been identified.

Nivelon clearly took great pains to produce a book that he wanted. There is no recorded publisher, and if a publisher was involved at an earlier date he must have been jettisoned, like Gravelot. Given the crafted quality of the whole production, there is every indication that the volume was a labour of love, that it took some time to produce and that the author was charting new waters. It must have been an expensive production which, in view of the scarcity of copies, must have lost money. However, the sale of copies may not have been Nivelon's main purpose, as he might have regarded the book primarily as equipment and promotion for his dancing school.

It has often been noted that the poses described by Nivelon appear in portraits painted during the middle years of the century by (to name but three) Arthur Devis, Francis Hayman and Thomas Gainsborough.[11] The poses in, for example, Devis's *Lady and Gentleman in a Landscape* of the later 1740s (fig. 4) demonstrate that many a member of the gentry would have adopted the kind of position illustrated in Nivelon's work. Indeed the ideas the book contains were commonplace and widely accepted. The purpose of the volume, and indeed a dancing master's class, was to propagate these manners to aspiring persons ("of what Condition so ever") throughout the country.

There is an interesting postscript which bears out this development. The text reappeared without alteration but with an addition concerning the "genteel and proper Use" of the fan in a book compiled by Matthew Towle in 1770, entitled *The Young Gentleman and Lady's Private Tutor in Three Parts*. The first Part concerns the "Moral and Social Duties &c viz. Piety, Wisdom, Prudence, Fortitude ...", the second "Of Behaviour to God, parents, Company ... [and] Servants ..." and the third "Behaviour in the Dancing School". The third section updates Dandridge's illustrations with cruder

70

5. George Langley Smith, *Walking*, from Matthew Towle, *The Young Gentleman and Lady's Private Tutor in Three Parts*, London 1770

images of models wearing contemporary dress in somewhat naive engravings by George Langley Smith (fig. 5).[12] At the front of the volume Towle states that the book will "improve the Minds and Morals of Youth". This statement heads a subscription list consisting of provincial schools, implying the educative desire to better pupils in society and provide a means to social acceptability – a somewhat deflating outcome, which leads in due course to the implications of the word 'genteel' today, as a pretension and affectation belying the very value desired.

Hugh Belsey
Gainsborough's House, Sudbury

The copy of Nivelon's book used for this edition is in the collection of Gainsborough's House, Sudbury. The purchase of the book was generously assisted by the Friends of the National Libraries in October 2002.

NOTES

1. *The Dancing-Master: or, The Art of Dancing Explained*, London 1728, Preface, p. VII [hereafter Essex 1728]. See further P.H. Highfill Jr, K.A. Burnim and E.A. Langhans, *A Biographical Dictionary of Actors ...*, 19 vols., Carbondale and Edwardsville (Illinois) 1973–93 [hereafter Highfill] and a re-translation of Rameau by C.W. Beaumont, *The Dancing Master*, London 1931. In his *Analysis of Beauty*, cited below, Hogarth, too, accepts the truism that dance was "the genius of the French nation" (though he goes on to prefer the Commedia dell'Arte).

2. Feuillet's book was translated into English by John Weaver as *Orchesography or, the Art of Dancing ... an Exact and Just Translation from the French of Monsieur Feuillet*, London 1706. John Essex (p. XX) remarks of John Weaver, "Our Profession in general are obliged to him for the many Proofs of his Knowledge, that are so many Helps to our Art, which in Reality he has rather made a Science". See further Highfill, V, pp. 95–97, and R. Ralph, *The Life and Works of John Weaver*, London 1985.

3. For instance the Wood family, who established a flourishing business in East Anglia: see H. Belsey, 'Thomas Gainsborough as an Ipswich Musician, a Collector of Prints and a Caricaturist', *East Anglia's History: Studies in Honour of Norman Scarfe*, Woodbridge and Norwich 2002, pp. 298–300.

4. Essex 1928, preface, p. VII. This work indeed includes instructions for deportment, such as making a bow and a curtsey.

5. *The Letters of Philip Dormer Stanhope, Earl of Chesterfield*, ed. John Bradshaw, 3 vols., London 1892, I, pp. 154–55, London, 27 September 1748. According to Samuel Johnson, Chesterfield's letters "inculcated the morals of a Strumpet and the Manners of a Dancing-master".

6. W. Hogarth, *The Analysis of Beauty*, ed. R. Paulson, New Haven and London 1997, p. 104.

7. Fuller biographies of the Nivelon family are provided by Highfill, II, pp. 33–36. The critique of Nivelon's dancing comes from this source (p. 34).

8. Illustrated in Highfill, IX, p. 118, *s.v.* Laguerre, Mrs John, Mary.

9. H.A. Hammelmann, 'A Georgian Guide to Deportment', *Country Life*, 16 May 1968, pp. 1272–73. For a comprehensive review of courtesy literature see J.E. Mason, *Gentlefolk in the Making: Studies in the History of English Courtesy Literature and related topics 1531 to 1774*, Philadelphia 1935.

10. Both are illustrated in E. Einberg, *The French Taste in English Painting*; exh. cat., Kenwood, 1968, no. 68, plates 3 and 4 [hereafter Kenwood 1968].

11. Kenwood 1968, no. 85, and E.G. D'Oench, *The Conversation Piece: Arthur Devis and His Contemporaries*, exh. cat., Yale Center for British Art, New Haven, 1980, no. 70.

12. Towle 1770, pp. 189ff., especially pp. 194–95.